★NSIDE ★NSYNC

THE ULTIMATE OFFICIAL ALBUM

★NSIDE ★NSYNC

THE ULTIMATE OFFICIAL ALBUM

BY ★NSYNC

WITH STEVE PREVESK & MELINDA BELL
ORIGINAL PHOTOGRAPHY BY TODD KAPLAN

UNIVERSE

Published in the United States of America in 1999 by Universe Publishing

A Division of Rizzoli International Publications, Inc., 300 Park Avenue South

New York, NY 10010

99 00 01 02 / 10 9 8 7 6 5 4 3 2 1

Printed in Canada

Library of Congress Catalog Card Number: 99-71280

Many thanks to Harry Markel of Fuji Photo Film U.S.A., Inc. for providing Fuji Professional Film for this book. For more information on FujiFilm, call 1-800-736-3600, extension 8815.

Thanks go out to Color Edge., Inc., located at 38 West 21st Street in New York City, (212) 633-6000, for providing the processing for the film used in this book.

**THIS IS DEDICATED
TO OUR MANY SUPPORTERS
THROUGHOUT THE YEARS, TO OUR
FAMILIES, FRIENDS, AND FANS.
WE LOVE YOU,
★NSYNC**

★*N*TRODUCTION

Seldom in the history of popular music has a single group captured the ears, hearts, and minds of a generation of fans as swiftly and energetically as *NSYNC has. Since April of 1998, when their hit single "I Want You Back" skyrocketed up the American music charts, their talent and infectious enthusiasm have been embraced by people of all ages and from every walk of life. *NSYNC has transcended the pop-star label to become something more, and through the energy and sincerity of their songs they have made a deep connection both to their devoted fans and to newcomers to the *NSYNC phenomenon.

Justin Randall Timberlake, James "Lansten" Lance Bass, Joshua Scott "JC" Chasez, Joseph "Joey" Anthony Fatone Jr., and Christopher "Chris" Alan Kirkpatrick all had a dream that someday they would be able to use their natural talents to entertain people. But they also had another priority: always to keep within sight the values that their parents had instilled in them. In the last couple of years, their longtime dream has come true, well beyond their wildest expectations. Yet through tedious rehearsals, long recording sessions, and a grueling schedule of performances and appearances, the guys still keep an eye on the things that really count: remaining best friends, staying close to their families, and of course, being loyal to millions of adoring fans. It is this special bond that seems to set them apart from so many other singers today. But how did a boyhood dream become such a dazzling reality? Actually, you could say it was *N the stars. . . .

A lot of hard work and a little good fortune combined to set in motion what quickly became a whirlwind of unexpected events. Here's a quick rundown of what happened. The boys, who had been jamming together for awhile, had cut a demo that found its way into the hands of Lou Pearlman of Trans Continental Entertainment. He was so impressed that he contacted Johnny Wright of Wright Entertainment Group. Johnny sensed that there was something special in the group's chemistry and set them up with a record contract with BMG in Germany. Their first hit, "I Want You Back," went gold in just a few months.

The enormous response overseas proved that this might be more than a one-time fluke: this had the makings of a bona fide phenomenon. Sure enough, "I Want You Back" went on to break the record for the fastest-rising single (originally set by Michael Jackson) and set another record for the longest reign for a new act on the charts. "Tearin' Up My Heart" quickly followed and propelled *NSYNC's debut album all the way to number one. The group's popularity soared and quickly spread across international borders. Their music, and the roar of growing legions of fans, could now be heard in the far corners of the world—from the United Kingdom to Mexico, from South Africa to Asia.

As overwhelming as their overseas success was to the guys of *NSYNC, they all knew deep down that the true test, the source of real satisfaction, would have to come from their home turf—America. After all, this was where their family and friends were; it's where they grew up and first got into music themselves. There was no doubt: the United States was truly where *NSYNC's success would be measured. What they quickly discovered was that to measure their success at home, they'd need a whole new yardstick: their debut album went platinum in just four months. Their dream—simply to perform together and entertain people—had not only been fulfilled; it had been surpassed well beyond their most outrageous fantasies. But wait a minute: These guys are just getting started!

Their future is as wide open as their imaginations—and among these five guys, there's no shortage of imagination. *NSYNC may still be flush with their success, but they realize that they have to come to terms with it. And they know that the one way to avoid getting carried away by it is to recognize the obligation they have to the very people who helped put them where they are today: their fans. Whether it's the electricity of a tour performance in a jam-packed arena or a one-to-one meeting with a disadvantaged child, every day is approached with one thing in mind: to give something back.

That's easy enough to say, but the challenge is to really do it. To understand this, you've got to get inside *NSYNC's world—climb on the tour bus, hang out with them during their down time, get up onstage to see what thirty-thousand screaming fans look like from the other side of the spotlight. What would it be like to be a part of their lives, to spend even a single day with Lance, Joey, Chris, JC, and Justin? *NSIDE *NSYNC lets you do just that: you'll get an up-close

and personal look at the guys through intimate images that most fans never get to see.

We'll walk you through an entire day of a concert tour—from tour bus to hotel to sound-check to final encore. You'll get a behind-the-scenes look at the hardworking and talented crew that make it all happen. Whether the guys are joking around backstage before the lights come up or having a quiet moment back at the hotel room, you'll be right there with them—from the moment they roll into town to the mad dash for the tour bus just after the show. So strap yourself in; you're about to have the time of your life—on tour with *NSYNC!

6:00 A.M. THE DAY'S ALREADY BEGUN . . .

It's a foggy, cool morning and while most people are still sound asleep, four tour buses quietly roll into town, headed for the arena. The arena is quiet: no screaming crowds, no pounding beats, no flashing cameras; but inside, the show has already begun. Actually, for Tim, the "show" began a long time ago. Tim is the tour's Production Manager and he has been preparing for the tour for months. Now that the four crew buses and eight trucks have arrived, Tim kicks into high gear: with his forty-three-person traveling crew and an additional eighty-four men and women hired locally, he begins to transform the empty arena into what will in a few hours be the site of an electrifying *NSYNC experience. The set carpenters start building the stage, the riggers are hooking up the fly track, the lighting grids are put into place, and the pyro crew prepares the explosives.

8:00 A.M. CATCHING THE LAST FEW WINKS . . .

Meanwhile, a few miles away, three more buses are headed into town; inside are the band, management, promoters, coordinators, and publicists who run the day-to-day operations of *NSYNC's tour. Melinda, of Wright Entertainment Group, along with Ibrahim and Fritz, make up *NSYNC's Tour Management Team. Cell phones and laptops close at hand, they're busy reviewing the day's itinerary for the guys with Doug, the management rep at home base in Orlando, Florida. Doug coordinates all requests from BMG and RCA from around the world and sends them out to the tour management and crew. Public appearances, meet-and-greets, travel schedules, radio and television spots, and the never-ending requests for tickets and backstage passes keep them in a constant but controlled frenzy. But where are the guys?

Away, for the moment at least, from ringing cell phones, the racket of stage construction, and the crush of press photographers, the boys of *NSYNC are on another bus headed directly for their hotel. Mornings are their precious down time and they're looking forward to a little peace and quiet before the day gets into full swing. As always, they're somewhat amazed to see a few fans in the hotel lobby when they arrive—how their fans know where to find them no matter where they go is still a mystery.

Having checked in, now is their chance to climb into bed in a quiet room and catch up on sleep, or if they were able to catch a few winks on the bus, maybe it's off to a local mall for some shopping. They're pretty much on their own but always seem to do things together. These are the moments that the guys cherish because they can really be themselves. They are just like any bunch of guys hanging out—except that for these five friends, millions of fans want to know their every move.

11:00 A.M. WHERE'S THAT IRON . . .

Back at the arena, the stage is starting to take shape. In the back hallways the production team is labeling dressing rooms, checking phone lines, and telling the caterers where lunch is to be served. Leslie, who handles the guys' wardrobe, is busy getting the performance outfits in order and sending out dry cleaning, making sure that *NSYNC look their best, as she does every night.

Nearby, *NSYNC's security chief, Randy (a.k.a. Big Dogg), reviews security procedures with Todd, Eric, Michael, Lonnie, Wesley, and Andre—*NSYNC's security team—to make sure that everything goes smoothly once the thousands of fans start pouring into the arena. Big Dogg and his team accompany the guys wherever they go—whether it's shopping in a mall or having lunch in a downtown café. When they're on tour, the guys in *NSYNC know they can let their guard down and chill, because Big Dogg and the fellas, when they're on duty at least, never do.

12:30 P.M. OKAY, ONE AT A TIME . . .

By lunchtime, the crew is sitting down to take a break from their hectic day, but for JC, Justin, Chris, Lance, and Joey, that's just when things start picking up; it's when they have to get ready to step into the public eye—where they'll be for the rest of the day and night. The guys know they're in demand, and with fame comes responsibility to the fans—and that means endless television appearances, radio interviews, autograph sessions, and public appearances. This is also the time when Big Dogg is busiest. His security team watches not only the guys but also their fans to make sure nothing gets out of hand, especially during public appearances when excited fans can get up close and pretty personal.

3:00 P.M. TESTING, TESTING. ONE, TWO, THREE . . .

Back at the arena the stage is up, the lights are hung, and everything looks ready, but the work is far from over. After a line check, *NSYNC's band—including Troy, Billy, Ruben, Paul, Byron, and musical director, Kevin—take the stage and begin jamming. It's sound-check time and mic levels and instruments must be meticulously adjusted to make sure that when the guys hit the stage and launch into their first song, the thousands of fans get the full-on *NSYNC experience. Meanwhile, things are warming up backstage: Ibrahim, Fritz, and Melinda get situated in their temporary offices and prepare for the frenzy that is about to take place.

Outside the arena, the air of excitement begins to intensify: fans start arriving, peeking in doors and windows hoping to get a glimpse of something—anything. The arena staff show up soon after and begin taking their places throughout the venue as concertgoers fill the parking lot and walkways surrounding the arena. Inside, the house lights are already being dimmed, and background music pumps through the arena as the anticipation outside becomes palpable.

5:00 P.M. HERE COMES ★NSYNC'S TOUR BUS!

The guys arrive at the venue and as always they are met by hundreds of fans who line the short route from the bus to the restricted area. They go directly to the dressing rooms, where catering has laid out some of their favorite drinks and snacks. Inside, the guys have no trouble keeping themselves busy: in between bites of food, they play video games, read fan mail, open presents, or play with Chris's dog, Busta. There's plenty of laughing and joking around to keep everybody loose. Spending a little time backstage with the guys before a show, soaking up their energy, you realize that performing is what they love to do most. And while they always seem comfortable with all the attention, you get the sense that they never really stop being surprised at, and thankful for, all their success.

In another room somewhere in the arena, the production crew, management team, and security staff meet with arena personnel to preview the night's show and make sure that everything is ready—that all the complicated elements that make a live *NSYNC performance work will come together perfectly. After that meeting, Melinda and the security team head to the will-call window to start coordinating what for some lucky fans, will be a night they'll never forget.

Meet-and-greet is a chance for a group of fans, who have either won a contest or have been invited by the tour to meet the guys in person. Once the fans present their passes and get inside the doors, they can hardly contain their excitement. They are led to large room; in front of them are five empty chairs and a long table with five magic markers. When the guys finally enter the room, the screams are ear-shattering. Eventually the guys, with the help of Big Dogg and his team, get everybody calmed down, at least to the point where fans can exchange a few words

with the bandmembers. Then everybody gets autographs from the group and is escorted back into the main part of the arena. Once outside the door, the looks on their faces say it all. For these fans, a few moments talking and hanging out with the guys has become the memory of a lifetime.

While the meet-and-greet keeps security and the bandmembers busy, it provides the exhausted production team a short breather. Often, they can be seen playing basketball on a hoop that is set up for them in a corridor backstage, or they might hang out in the catering room watching a ballgame on television.

6:30 P.M. FRONT ROW SEATS . . .

Finally, after months of anticipation on the part of the fans, the moment has arrived: arena staff, having received the go-ahead from the event managers, open the doors of the building, and thousands of fans begin pouring in. Some head for the T-shirt and concession stands, but most seem eager to find their seats—which, of course, won't get much use tonight.

7:00 P.M. OPENING ACTS TO THE STAGE . . .

The houselights go down, and by this time adrenaline is pumping on both sides of the stage. The opening band takes their places and kicks into their set, keeping the crowd's energy level fully peaked. Backstage the guys are in their dressing rooms as the management team works the

phones, still ringing with ticket and media requests. The production team settles in for some dinner.

It's around this time that the guys in *NSYNC get to hang out, as they do at most of their gigs, with some of the celebrities who happen to be in town and have come to check out the show. Some of the biggest names in the sports and entertainment industries walk down the halls with their families to say hi to the guys. For JC, Justin, Chris, Lance, and Joey it's still easy to get over-whelmed during these visits, since they often feel more like fans than celebrities themselves. The variety and enthusiasm of the people who come to see their shows never ceases to amaze them.

7:30 P.M. ALMOST SHOWTIME!

As the opening acts begin to wind down, Jennifer gets the fellas into hair and makeup. That done, it's off to wardrobe to get into their opening outfits. Outside, as the crew prepares the now darkened stage for the main attraction, the crowd's excitement builds, and what had been a buzz at the beginning of the night has grown into a near-roar. The fans can sense the time is near.

Backstage, there's a brief moment of calm before the storm. Like athletes before a big game, the guys each have their own way of getting psyched up for the show, yet they all share the same intense combination of butterflies and raw excitement. These are the moments when they realize the huge responsibility they have to their fans, but they know they can count on each other to give the best show possible. Everyone huddles for a short prayer, giving thanks for the talents and opportunities they have been given, then it's hugs to everyone, and with an enthusiastic shout, they head for the stage . . . it's showtime!

8:00 P.M. LADIES AND GENTLEMEN, ★NSYNC!

You don't have to be inside the arena to know that *NSYNC just took the stage. The deafening roar of the fans seems to shake a whole city block. The opening number pulsates, and spotlights blaze down on each of the five singers, sending the crowd into a frenzy. This is what all the trouble was for—all the preparations, promotions, coordination: It's all about the performance, the one thing all five guys in the group live for when they're on tour.

For all the raucous excitement in the arena and onstage, this is one of the few moments when some of the tour's behind-the-scenes players can chill for a bit and start planning for the next big event. Now that the guys are onstage, the show has begun, and ticket requests are taken care of, Fritz, Melinda, and Ibrahim, along with the management team, begin to work on the next tour date and try to catch up on some personal things, like phone calls to family and friends.

8:45 P.M. QUICK! GET ME THAT SHIRT!

Right now, Big Dogg and his security team are watching every move, Gary is controlling the dazzling light displays you see onstage, Tim is mixing the sound, David is in monitor world, Anthony manages the stage, while backstage, Leslie and Jennifer hustle the guys in and out of six wardrobe and hair and makeup changes.

10:00 P.M. HOUSELIGHTS UP!

As the show nears its electrifying climax, preparations have already been made to get the band safely out of the arena after

the lights go down. Members of the security team take their positions at several checkpoints along a designated exit route, just as the bandmembers can be heard shouting their final "thank you" into the mics, and the crowd's roar swells and shakes the foundations of the arena. The lights are down, and the guys run for the ramp that takes them directly offstage. From there the security team directs them with flashlights through the corridors of the arena and out into the back parking lot, where they quickly jump on the bus—still in costume—and head for the next city.

As the last fans trickle out of the arena, there is still a bristling energy in the air, even with the houselights up. As soon as the show ends, Anthony, the stage manager, can be heard giving directions as to what goes where. The production team gets back to work taking down the stage and packing everything up. Outside in the parking lot, the crowd disperses, still fully amped from the show.

2:00 A.M. ZZZzzz . . .

Finally, the last box is loaded onto the last truck and a tired crew boards the buses. They unwind by talking about the day's work and how the show went, but sleep comes quickly, for tomorrow they know they have to do it all over again.

For JC, Justin, Chris, Lance, and Joey, another show is over and it is on to the next one. It is then, in those quiet moments alone, that the group realizes they are part of a bigger family—one that works together, laughs together, and sometimes even cries together—all with one goal in mind. That goal is to make sure that when fans leave an *NSYNC concert, they can say they saw the best.

LET

"MY FRIEND JONAH CREATED THE MONSTER FOR THIS INTRO. WE LIKE TO INCORPORATE OUR FRIENDS INTO THE SHOW WHENEVER WE CAN."
—JOEY

THE SHOW

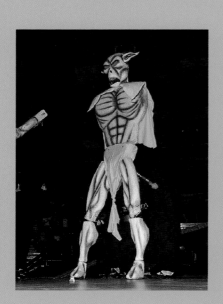

BEGIN . . . .

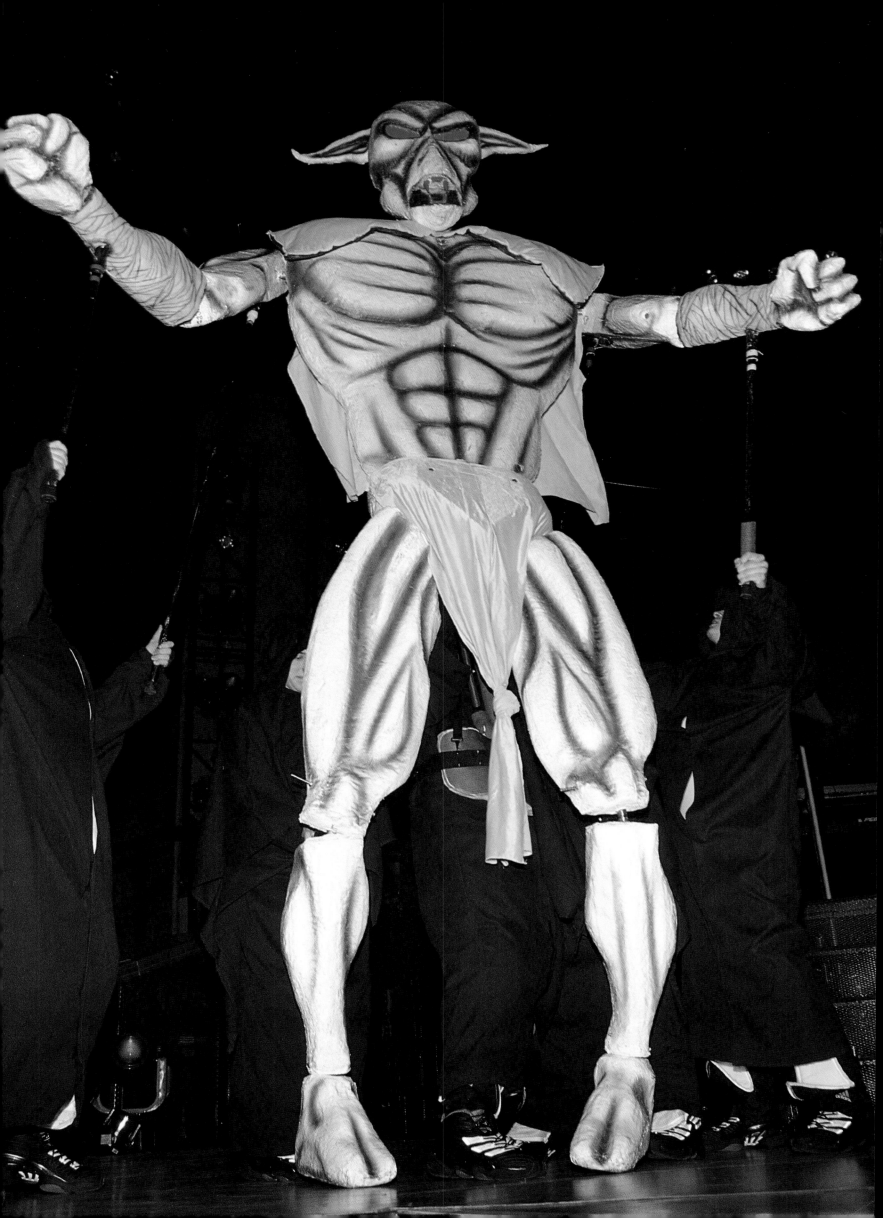

CAN YOU GUESS

WHO'S WHO?

HEARING THE FANS GETS US PUMPED UP EVERY TIME.

YESYESYES

★NSYNC HAS

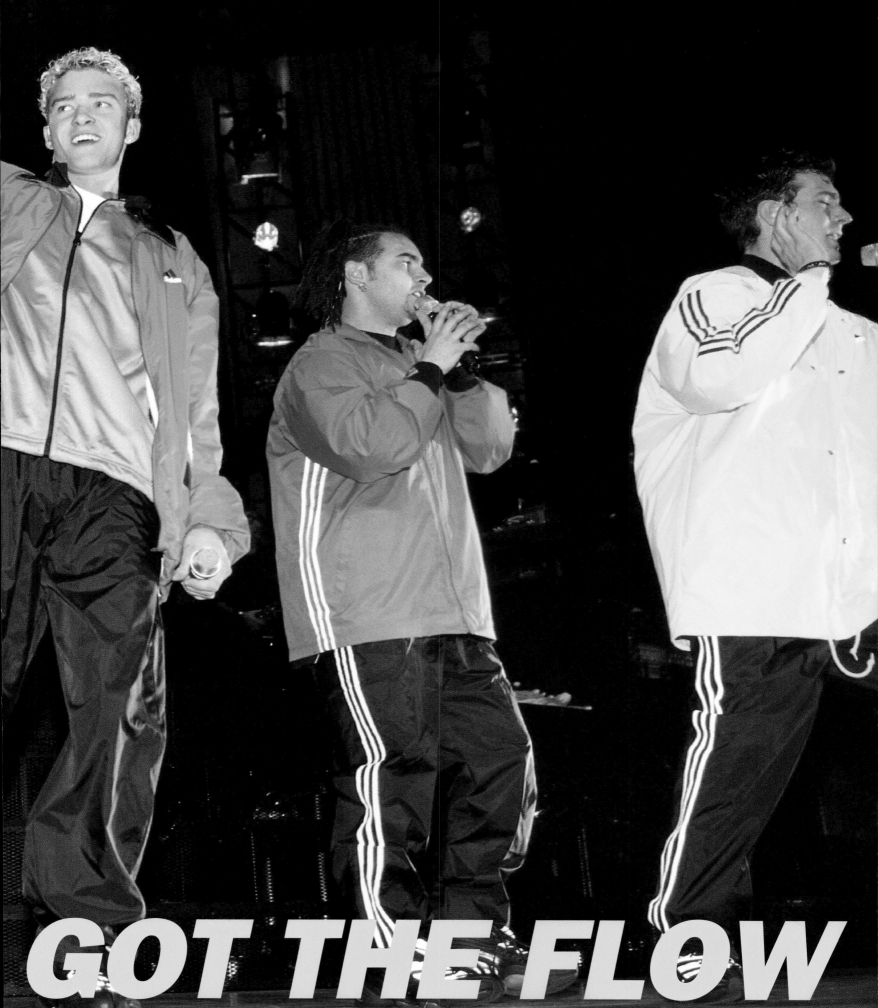

"BEFORE EVERY SHOW I GO THROUGH THE SAME WARM-UP ROUTINE TO PREPARE FOR WHEN I TAKE THE STAGE." —JUSTIN

WE DON'T HAVE TO GO TO A GYM TO WORK OUT.

PERFORMING

KEEPS US IN SHAPE.

WE'D BRING EVERYONE UP ONSTAGE
IF WE

FROM THE FIRST TIME I WAS UP ON STAGE I WAS HOOKED.

MUSIC HISTORY 101

WE START OUR HISTORY IN THAT DECADE OF LOVE

THE '60s

WE CHOSE "THAT THING YOU DO" TO SHOWCASE THE '60s AND WE DECIDED TO PLAY THE INSTRUMENTS OURSELVES TO MAKE THE NUMBER MORE REALISTIC.

MUSIC HISTORY GROOVES

INTO THE '70s

THE DECADE WOULDN'T BE COMPLETE WITHOUT THE *JACKSONS.*

THE CURLS?

WE'VE HAD VISITS FROM MARLON, TITO, AND JANET —AND THEY'VE ALL BEEN THRILLED WITH OUR TRIBUTE TO THEM.

MUSIC HISTORY ROLLS INTO
THE '80s

A DECADE OF . . . CELEBRATION!

JOEY'S PARTIES ARE NEVER

COMPLETE WITHOUT **CONFETTI**

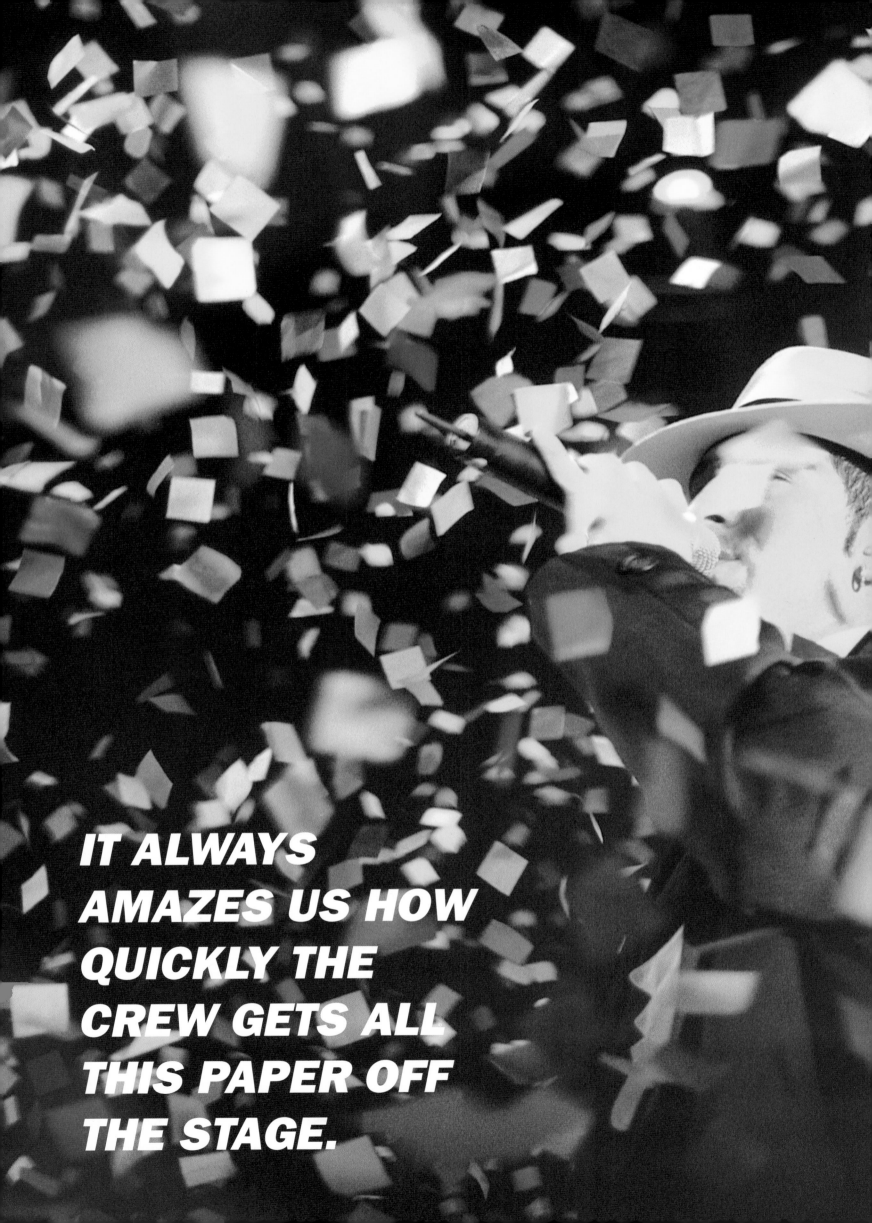

IT ALWAYS
AMAZES US HOW
QUICKLY THE
CREW GETS ALL
THIS PAPER OFF
THE STAGE.

AND THE '90s
IN

*NSYNC MAKES MUSIC HISTORY!

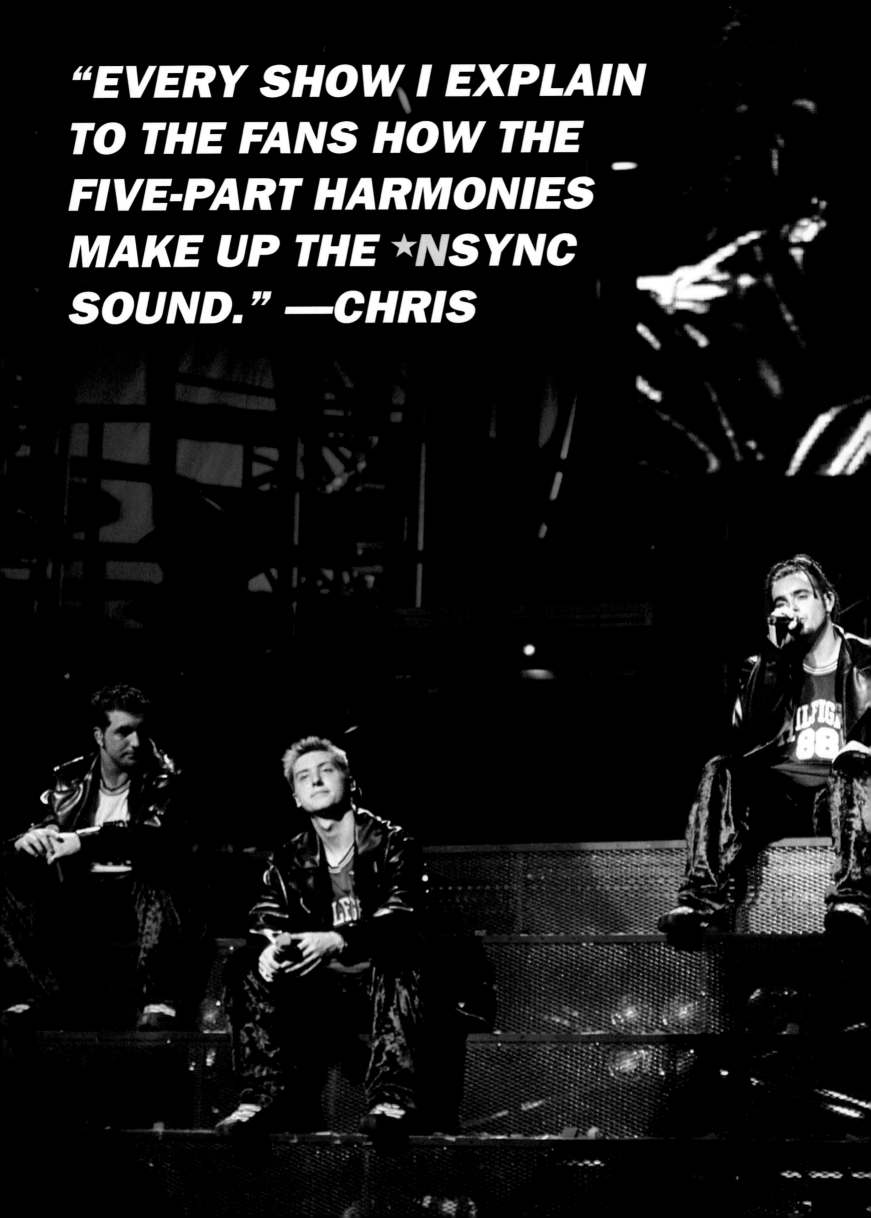

"EVERY SHOW I EXPLAIN TO THE FANS HOW THE FIVE-PART HARMONIES MAKE UP THE ★NSYNC SOUND." —CHRIS

"SOMETIMES I STILL CAN'T BELIEVE OUR SUCCESS."
—LANCE

"'I JUST WANNA BE WITH YOU' IS ONE OF MY FAVORITE CHOREOGRAPHED SONGS. WE WORK HARD TO PERFECT OUR DANCE MOVES."
—JOEY

TELL ME, CAN

THIS BE REAL?

"THE GUYS JOKE THAT SOME NIGHT
THEY'RE JUST GOING TO LEAVE THE STAGE
'CAUSE I HOLD THE END OF 'GOD MUST
HAVE SPENT A LITTLE MORE TIME ON YOU'
FOR SO LONG." —JUSTIN

A SHOW WOULDN'T
BE COMPLETE
WITHOUT THE SONG
THAT STARTED IT
ALL . . .

I WANT Y

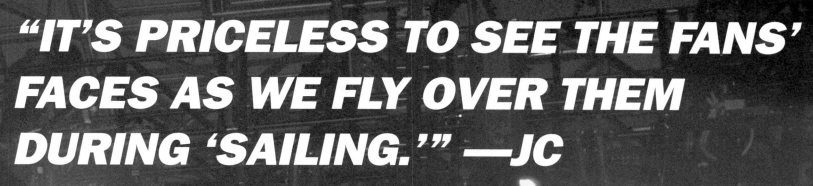

"IT'S PRICELESS TO SEE THE FANS'
FACES AS WE FLY OVER THEM
DURING 'SAILING.'" —JC

IN THE BEGINNING FLYING MADE US A LITTLE NERVOUS.

NOW ... IT'S

AWESOME

OUR ADRENALINE KEEPS US GOING THE ENTIRE SHOW . . .

. . . BY THE END WE'RE SO PUMPED

THAT IT'S HARD TO GO TO SLEEP.

IT'S

COOL...

. . . TO GET UP CLOSE TO MORE FANS THAN JUST THOSE IN THE FRONT ROW.

BACKSTAGE

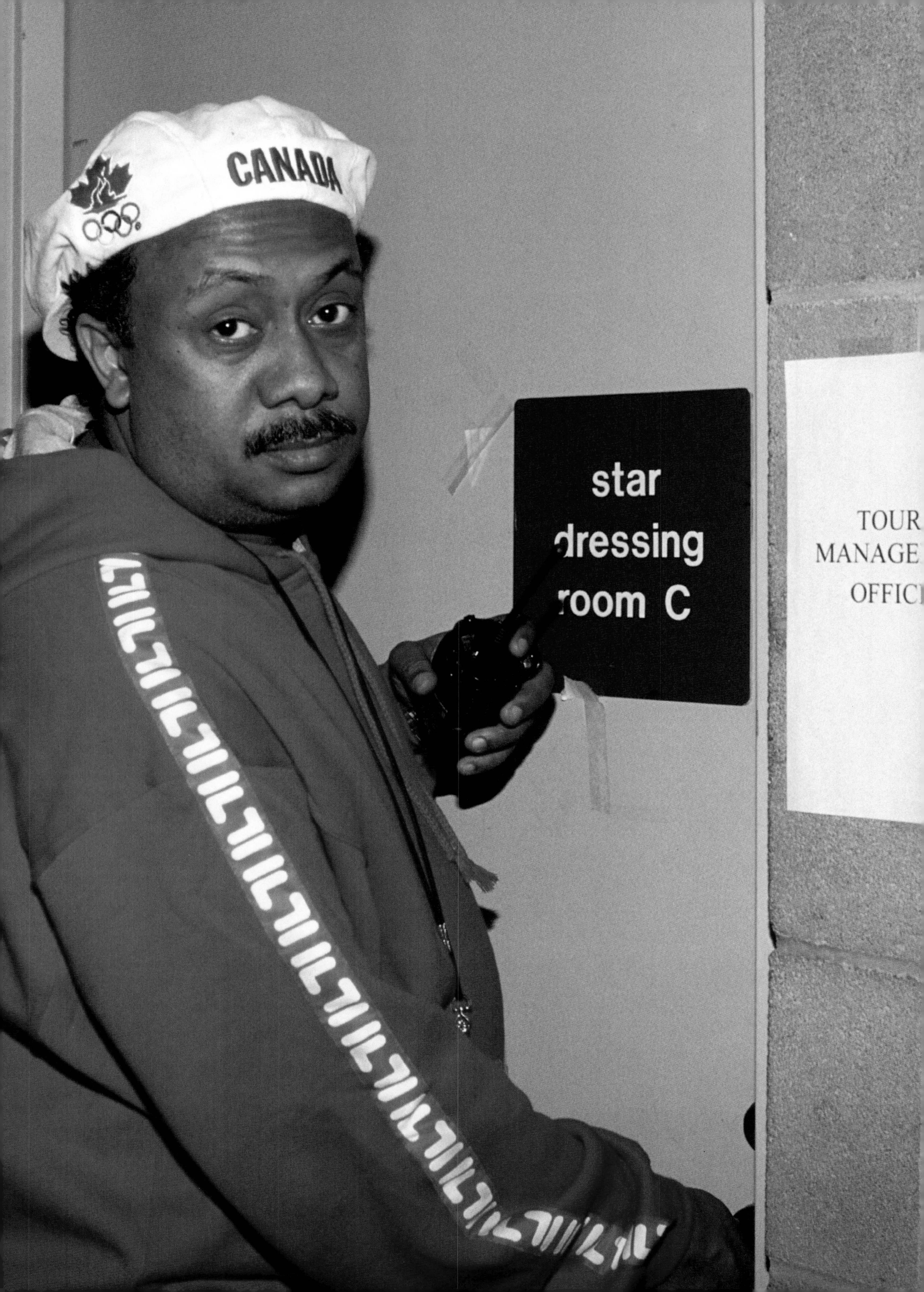
CANADA
star
dressing
room C
TOUR
MANAGE
OFFIC

EVEN WHEN WE'RE NOT ONSTAGE WE'RE STILL REALLY VISIBLE IN

THE

PUBLIC EYE

"IT TAKES HOURS TO GET MY HAIR BRAIDED. SOMETIMES I'M SO TIRED I FALL ASLEEP IN THE CHAIR." —CHRIS

"EVERY CHANCE I GET I TRY TO READ E-MAIL FROM FANS."
—CHRIS

THE BIG DOGG

ERIC, A.K.A.
BIG "E"

LONNIE, A.K.A.
BUNDY

RANDY, A.K.A.
BIG DOGG

POSSE

WES

ANDRE, A.K.A.
PRETTY TONY

TODD, A.K.A.
SLIM

RUBEN

KEVIN

BILLY

TROY

THE BAND

WE SET UP A VIP SECTION AT EACH SHOW FOR OUR SPECIAL GUESTS.

I'VE FALLEN AND

"YOU'VE GOT TO HAVE A SENSE OF HUMOR TO KEEP YOUR SANITY." —LANCE

I CAN'T GET UP!

TIM, WHO U WIT?

JOEY THANKS LESLIE FOR SEW
THE RIP IN HIS PANTS.

WHO DOES MELINDA CALL WHEN
SECURITY ATTACKS?

JOHNNY AND ANTHONY GO OVER NOTES
WITH THE GUYS DURING REHEARSAL.

GENIUS AT WORK . . . JOHNNY WRIGHT

"I KNOW I'M IN GOOD HANDS. LONNIE'S LIKE MY BIG (VERY BIG) BROTHER." —JUSTIN

EVEN AFTER PERFORMING HUNDREDS OF TIMES, THE NERVES STILL KICK IN WHEN WE PUT ON OUR COSTUMES AND EAR MONITORS BEFORE THE OPENING NUMBER.

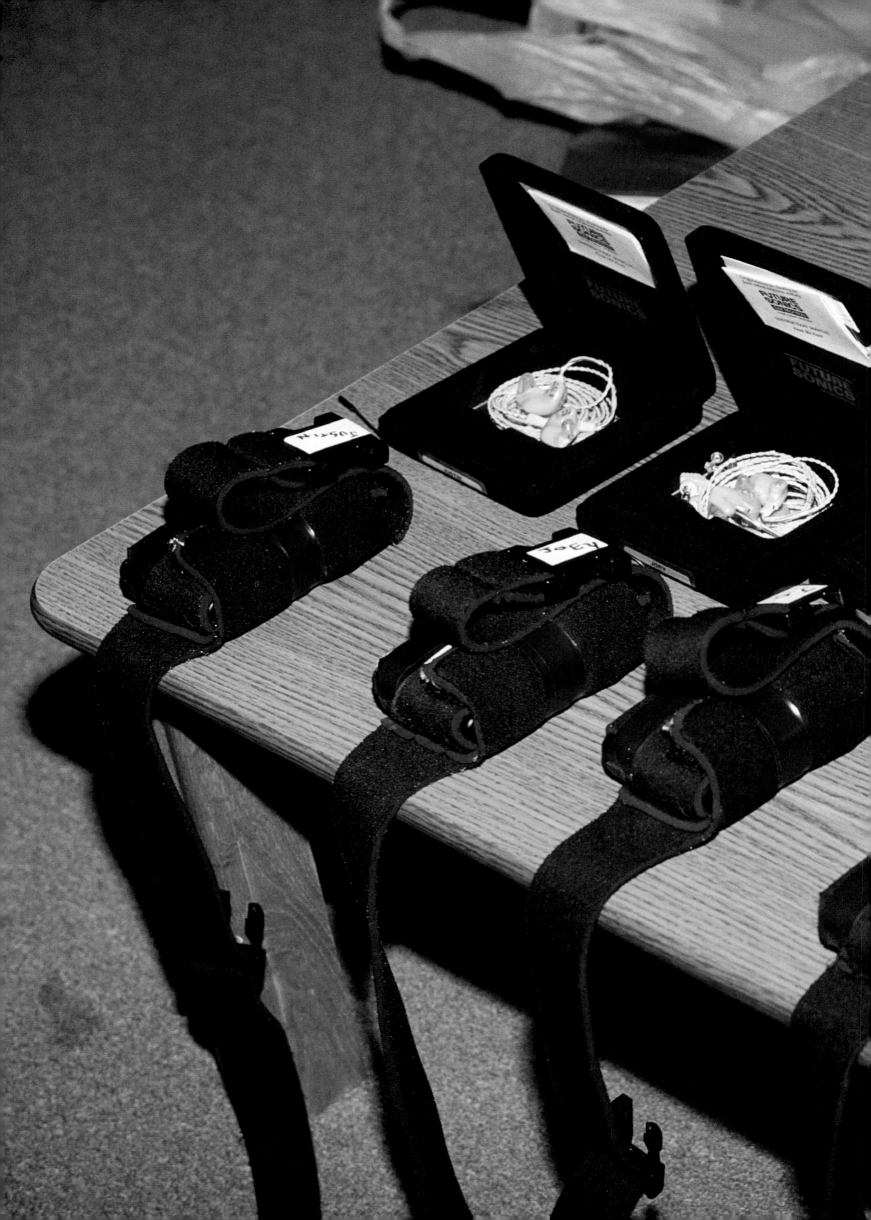

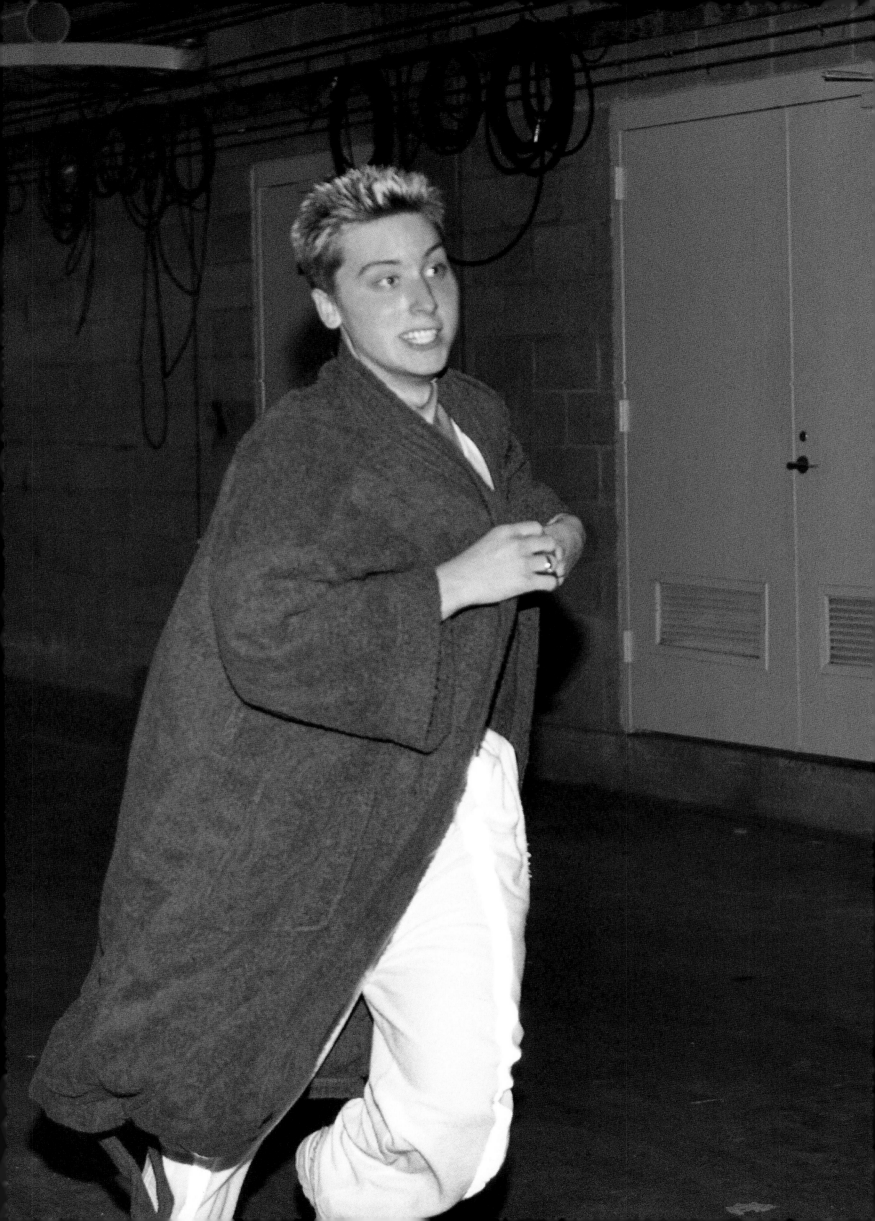

FORGET BIG DOGG . . .

I'M THE REAL BIG DOG ON THIS TOUR.

ME AND MY BUDDY BUSTA

WE CAN'T WORK

ALL THE TIME

FAMILY RESEMBLANCE? JOEY AND HIS BROTHER, STEVE.

BILLY GIVING JOEY A QUICK DRUM LESSON.

SITTIN' ON TOP

SOMETIMES IT'S GOOD TO JUST CHILL OUT AND AMUSE EACH OTHER.

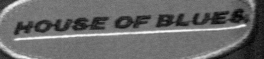

IS FUNDAMENTAL

EATING IS AN ESSENTIAL PART OF OUR DAY. OUR BUS IS ALWAYS STOCKED WITH TONS OF FOOD.

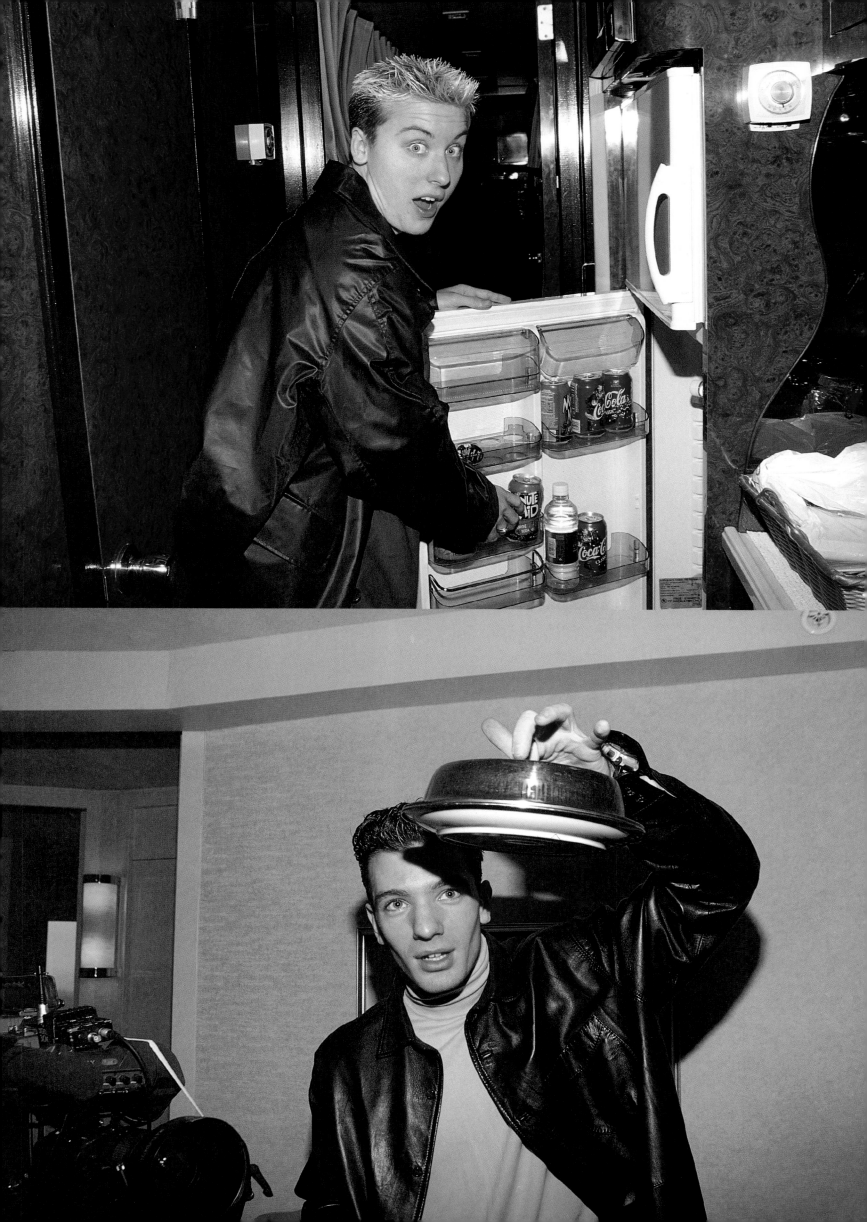

YOU WANT

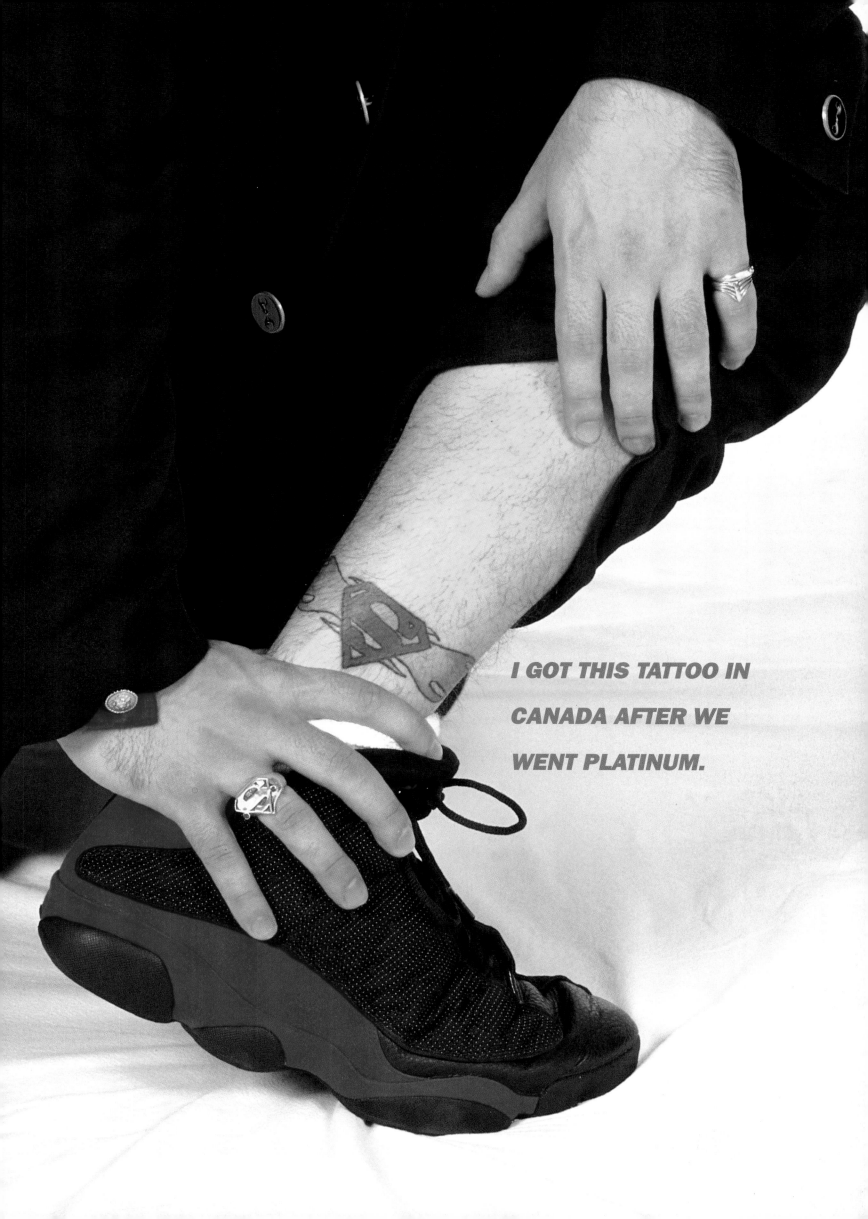

I GOT THIS TATTOO IN CANADA AFTER WE WENT PLATINUM.

"I'VE GOTTEN USED TO SLEEP-ING ON THE BUS. NOW I ALMOST LIKE IT BETTER THAN SLEEPING IN A HOTEL BED." —LANCE

ICE . . . BABY

SO HERE'S JOEY'S LUGGAGE.

WHERE'S EVERYBODY ELSE'S?

TOURING IS AN INCREDIBLE WHIRLWIND OF SCREAMING FANS, COSTUME CHANGES, SOUND CHECKS, AND NIGHTS ON BUSES. WE WOULDN'T TRADE ANY OF IT FOR THE WORLD.

THE EXTENDED

*NSYNC

Justin Timberlake	*Artist*
Chris Kirkpatrick	*Artist*
Joey Fatone	*Artist*
Lance Bass	*Artist*
JC Chasez	*Artist*
Darrin Henson	*Show Choreographer*

*NSYNC BAND

Kevin Antunes	*Musical Director/Keyboards*
Troy Antunes	*Bass*
William Ashbaugh	*Drums*
Byron Chambers	*Keyboards*
Paul Howard	*Horns & Percussion*
Ruben Ruiz	*Guitar*

EXCLUSIVE MANAGEMENT

Wright Entertainment Group, Orlando, FL

Johnny Wright	*Manager & Show Producer*
Doug Brown	*Artist Management Rep*
Melinda Jay Bell	*Special Projects Producer*
Yasmine Ballister	*Stylist*

Trans Continental Records, Inc., Orlando, FL
Lou Pearlman, *Executive Director*
Greg Augustyniak, *Director of Merchandising*

PERSONAL SECURITY TEAM

Randy Jones	*Director of Security*
Todd Dukes	*Chief of Security*
Eric Burrows	
Michael Greaves	
Lonnie Jones	
Wesley Long	
Andre Persons	

TOURING PERSONNEL

Ibrahim Duarte	*Tour Manager*
Tim Miller	*Production Manager/FOH Engineer*
Florence Tse	*Production Assistant*
Rob Schlotman	*Tour Accountant*
Fritz Maugile	*Road Manager*
Anthony Giordano	*Stage Manager*
Bob Mullin	*Head Carpenter*
Dave Brooks	*Monitor Engineer*
David Moncrieffe	*Sound Crew Chief*
Steve Cohen	*Lighting & Set Designer*
Gary Waldie	*Lighting Director*
Storm Sollars	*Lighting Crew Chief*
Chuck Melton	*Head Rigger*
David Davidian	*Video Director*
James Bump	*Monitor Technician*
John Keith	*Audio Technician*
Bobby Savage	*Rigger*
Dale Long	*Rigger*
Mark Ward	*Branam Fly Rig*
Lance Bogan	*Branam Fly Rig*

Curtis Baker	*Carpenter*
Tim Shannahan	*Carpenter*
Steve Aleff	*Pyro Technician*
Arnold Serame	*Lighting Programmer*
Bob Fry	*Lighting Technician*
Mark Swartz	*Lighting Technician*
Sean Carrico	*Lighting Technician*
Bob Longo	*Backline Technician*
Billy Brett	*Backline Technician*
Steve Crain	*Backline Technician*
Jon Huntington	*Video Engineer*
Redo Jackson	*Video Technician*
Robbie Alvarez	*Video Technician*
Bert Pare	*Video Technician*
Greg Frederick	*Jumbotron Technician*
Steve Fatone	*Staff Videographer*
Jennifer Currie	*Hair & Makeup*
Leslie Ramos	*Wardrobe*
Fred Rogers	*Costumer*
Nancy Bergman	*Massage Therapist*

BUS DRIVERS / TRUCK DRIVERS

BUS DRIVERS	TRUCK DRIVERS
Leon Blue	David Desaulniers
Harry Commons	Eric Peterson
James Forges	Troy Cross
Kenny Forges	Sharon Cross
Gail Corby	Dale Carriveau
Mark McBride	Chris De Korte
	Gary Lambert
	Sammy Mendez

BOOKING AGENT

Renaissance Entertainment
David Zedeck, Cheryl Corbin

RECORD LABEL

RCA Records / USA
New York, NY
BMG / International

FAN CLUB INFORMATION

Official ★NSYNC International Fan Club
P.O. Box 5248
Bellingham, WA 98227
Contact: Gerri Karr

OFFICIAL WEBSITE

www.nsync.com

SPECIAL THANKS GO TO:

The Attic
FILA Sports, Inc.
LU Kyle Young Clothing
National Basketball Association
National Football League
Nike
Reebok International

TATYANA ALI
DRESSING ROOM

←

TOUR
MANAGEMENT
OFFICE

←

'N SYNC
BAND

←

'N SYNC
WARDROBE

←

'N SYNC
DRESSING
ROOM

←

CATERING

←

N SYNC
PRODUCTION
OFFICE

→

**TODAY'S SCHEDULE
CHAPEL HILL, NC
SATURDAY, MARCH 6, 1999**

4:00 PM	LINE CHECK
4:30 PM	N SYNC BAND SOUNDCHECK
5:00 PM	N SYNC SOUNDCHECK
5:30 PM	FINISH N SYNC SOUNDCHECK
N/A	TATYANA, B*WITCHED SOUNDCHECK
6:00 PM	DOORS
7:00 PM	SHOW CALL
	SPOTS GO UP
7:30-7:50P	B*WITCHED
7:50-8:10P	TATYANA ALI
8:30-10P	'N SYNC
10:00 PM	CREW CALL BACK

THANKS AND GOOD NIGHT.